POC

Around
Melton Mowbray

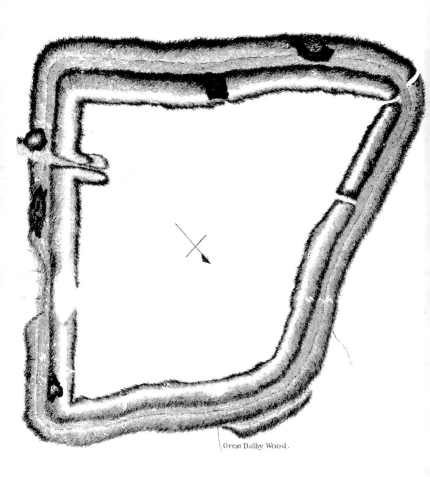

Great Dalby Wood.

A plan of the Iron Age encampment on top of Burrough Hill drawn in May 1796 by
I. Tailby. This hill-fort of the Iron Age (c. 600 BC–AD 43) is one of the most visited
archaeological sites in Leicestershire. It dominates the Jurassic escarpment overlooking
the Wreake Valley to the south-east of Melton Mowbray, and can be seen from many high
vantage points in two-thirds of all the places listed in this publication.

POCKET IMAGES

Around
Melton Mowbray

Trevor Hickman

NONSUCH

First published 1992
This new pocket edition 2007
Images unchanged from first edition

Nonsuch Publishing Limited
Cirencester Road, Chalford,
Stroud, Gloucestershire, GL6 8PE
www.nonsuch-publishing.com

Nonsuch Publishing is an imprint of NPI Media Group

© Trevor Hickman, 1992

The right of Trevor Hickman to be identified as the Author
of this work has been asserted in accordance with the
Copyrights, Designs and Patents Act 1988.

British Library Cataloguing in Publication Data.
A catalogue record for this book is available from the British Library.

ISBN 978-1-84588-424-6

Typesetting and origination by NPI Media Group
Printed in Great Britain

Contents

Introduction

When I am visiting various parts of England and discussion develops concerning my home town I find the immediate response is normally, 'Oh, that's where pork pies come from', or 'the centre for Stilton cheese' and, sometimes, 'Yes! that's where fox-hunting commenced.' Most people living in this area of the country would agree with all three of these comments. What I have attempted to do in this book is to gather together old photographs that in some way depict our local interests, industry and what has happened over the last one hundred years in the Melton Mowbray district. It is my personal collection, for which I take full responsibility; there are glaring omissions throughout the book, often because I have not been able to locate a suitable photograph, and there are also restraints in producing a book such as this on how many photographs can be used.

During the early spring of 1992 I visited each parish listed on the plan printed on p. 4. In driving around this beautiful part of England with nothing better to do than look at the landscape and position ninety-year-old photographs into their present day setting, I noticed a number of features projected in sharp relief: the splendid panoramic variation of shades of green spreading before me; quaint stone-built villages nestling in the fold of a low sloping hill; the brown face of the stone cottages blending in with the lush green of the fields and trees. Out towards the Vale of Belvoir and the Lincolnshire flat lands strange brown cliffs of sandstone run along field headlands, a legacy of opencast ironstone mining in this part of Leicestershire. After Stilton cheese, pork pies and hunting, the production of iron ore was a major factor in providing employment for villagers in this area from the end of the nineteenth century to the 1950s. In my youth I was fascinated by the small gauge railway system operating on the edge of the Vale of Belvoir, and the drag lines with cabins that looked like half-timbered buildings and dotted the landscape around Buckminster and Sewstern. With the help of my late father-in-law and my miller friend from Whissendine Mill I have included photographs recording this chapter of the Industrial Revolution as it affected this area some thirty years ago. Some of the photographs are poor quality; because it was such an everyday occurrence to see opencast mining near your village very few people photographed the system. Even though the countryside was ripped apart, redevelopment of the land has been superbly carried out and in many instances it is very difficult to see where the mining took place as the hedges have been replanted, repeating the rectangular field system so important to the economy of this area.

As the eighteenth-century enclosure awards began to take effect, and the large open fields were broken up into smaller hedged units, so farming methods changed. The lush grass meadows that gradually developed in the hawthorne-hedged enclosures witnessed the introduction of the herds of milking cows that produce excellent creamy milk so necessary to produce fine cheese. So cream cheese manufacture developed. It is presumed that some enterprising wife of a local farmer allowed some of her cream cheese to mature long beyond its normal 'shelf-life', thereby allowing the introduction of the grey-green mould so important in good prime Stilton. When and where did Stilton cheese originate? In my opinion it happened some time during the early part of the eighteenth century, almost certainly by accident. The earliest recorded account of its manufacture suggests it could have been made in the farm kitchen of Quenby Hall. There is hardly a village around Melton Mowbray that did not have a farmer making Stilton cheese, and most village historians state that it was made in their village first. Certainly it was made in very large quantities by the Pawletts of Wymondham at the middle of the eighteenth century and the early part of the nineteenth century, and later by the Morris family of Scalford and Wymondham who certainly marketed the product in large quantities. Their cheese was sold in the village of Stilton on the Great North Road. A cream cheese, however, was being sold at The Bell Inn, Stilton long before the Pawletts were producing it. In the production of Stilton large surpluses of whey are created, which was mixed with recycled waste food and corn products to form 'swill', an excellent feed for pigs. Stilton cheese manufacturers normally farmed pigs, in sties adjacent to the dairy, for their bacon and ham which was salted down for subsequent use. On slaughtering the animals a considerable quantity of surplus pork was always available. This was used in pork pies, brawn and chitterlings among other products. There was hardly a cottage in this area of Leicestershire that did not fatten up a pig, the piglet having been purchased from the local dairy. Most kitchen shelves carried a whole range of wooden pork pie moulds. There was more than one farming unit incorporating a windmill where the miller provided the flour, the farmer's wife produced cheese, and adjacent pigsties provided pork for the pies that were baked on site in the large kitchen oven along with bread, all for general sale.

To provide good grazing land and to enclose the cows that produced such fine milk in this area, thick, well maintained hawthorn hedges are needed. On enclosing the large fields, small areas of wasteland were left. These developed into the spinneys that are dotted around the landscape, linking the field system together, and provided an ideal breeding ground for foxes. The spinneys provided the cover for the foxes' earths and the hedges provided an exellent system of covered trackways to allow this cunning animal access, under cover, to new hunting grounds. Having no natural enemies, the fox multiplied, and farmers had no choice but to hunt it down. The easiest method was with a pack of hounds and so, as part of the necessary control of a pest that killed large quantities of poultry and young lambs, fox-hunting developed into a spectacular rural sport. Thus the landscape was maintained for centuries, supporting the farmers' needs and providing excellent jumps for the sporting fraternity with sufficient private funds who could indulge in this activity. The season was spent in Melton Mowbray, fine houses being built to meet the needs of the huntsmen. Hunting had many spin-offs: the sport provided considerable employment, and the locally produced cheese and pies were enjoyed by the huntsmen as well as the local population. Vast quantities were exported out of the area, and the manufacture of such products soon became a major industry in this part of the country.

Among this collection I have included photographs of people wherever possible, for without people we would have no record. After all, the part of the country in which we live is a man-made landscape. In a very short space of time, however, nature covers up the scars that we leave on the landscape by farming, industrial and military use. In my lifetime what were areas of dereliction have become listed sites of special scientific interest because of the wildlife that has returned—a fine example is Saltby Heath—and that is how it should be.

My collection is a pictorial record of this part of Leicestershire, and a contribution to the wealth of material already published, not a new idea. John Throsby, a local historian and artist, published his select views in 1789, and many other artists have done the same since that date, including Rigby Graham, who published his Leicestershire in 1980. Photography is a more accurate method but the artist often records features that the camera cannot see. That is why I have included a few photographs of various artists' impressions of the landscape in this book. All local history publications should be viewed together for what they are, bearing in mind that an individual or group will give its own interpretation of the features it has chosen to record. Not to be viewed in isolation, these publications present to the reading public a combined record of the countryside as the collectors see and observe it. This collection complements other publications of a similar type.

The major part of this collection is made up of photographs taken between the years 1900 and 1920, the golden age of photographic postcards. Very many of these photographs were sold as postcards, stamped with a halfpenny stamp, posted with the certain knowledge that it would arrive the next day. The messages written on the reverse are very interesting. Often they relate to the view on the face side and in some instances I have used this source material in compiling the captions in this book. Who were these early photographers? Many were employed by national and local agencies, and in this part of Leicestershire we had one outstanding photographer, W. Till, who worked on his own. Many of the early twentieth-century postcards reproduced here have his name on the face side. He travelled around the district on his bicycle, set up his plate camera on a tripod, selected the view, released the shutter and so recorded the scene. On returning to his studio in Melton Mowbray the glass plate was developed, and he then scratched his name and the title in reverse on the emulsion side of the plate and made one direct contact print. On returning to the location where the photograph was taken, days or even weeks later, he then attempted to sell further copies of the scene. In many instances he was not successful and only one print was made, thus explaining the rarity value of some early photographic postcards. Some of the views published in this book are reproductions of such scarce postcards. I trust the reader will enjoy them and that they will reach a wider audience than they were originally intended for.

Trevor Hickman
June 1992

One

Melton Mowbray

South Parade, c. 1900, showing J.W. Warner's lending library, printing and bookbinding establishment along with the stationery department and general bookshop on the left.

Thorpe End, Melton Mowbray.

The White Hart public house on Thorpe End, c. 1908.

Melton Mowbray cattle market in 1907.

The Market Place in the centre of town in 1935.

Outside Leonard Gill's ironmongery shop in the 'Barnes Block' in 1908.

The cheese fair in the 1890s, with Stilton cheeses stacked on the cobbles in the Market Place prior to their being auctioned off.

A typical Melton Mowbray family group of the 1930s, posing outside No. 64 Salisbury Avenue in 1937. Back row, left to right: Judith Pulford, Fred Pulford, Jane Pulford, Louisa Burton, David Burton, Arthur Burton. Second row: Margaret Sansby, Alice Sansby, Jean Pulford, John Pulford.

The teaching staff of Melton Modern Boys School, Limes Avenue in 1952. Of the twenty-four people shown, twenty-one are identified, in alphabetical order: Messrs Anderson, Barnett, Bartlett, Berry, Cullen, Fox, J.V. Fox, Greaves, Greenslade, Greenway, Goode, Hirst, Jackson, Kaye, Mayo, Neal, Parrott, Rowell, Till, Timms, Troll.

The Northern railway station being demolished in 1967.

The Midland railway station in 1910.

Burton Street, showing the Boat Inn on the right, in 1900.

Burton Street Basin in the 1880s. The Boat Inn is on the right.

The 1936 Hospital Gala, showing the parade passing down Nottingham Street.

A 1930 straight eight supercharged Bugatti standing outside Toad Hall off Burton Street, near the Boat Inn.

16

Brook Street, November 1940. A lone German bomber strafed Sherard Street with machine-gun fire and dropped a bomb that landed in Scalford Brook between Regent Street and Brook Street killing one man and causing damage to surrounding properties.

Sherard Street and Thorpe End, flooded in August 1922. Compare this photograph with the one reproduced on p. 10.

The Limes, off Sherard Street, before the First World War. Woolworths store now stands on this site.

The Melton Breadfast photograph of an engraving by C.G. Lewis after a painting by Sir Francis Grant PRA. From left to right: Massey Stanley, Earl of Wilton, Count Matuscewitz, Lord Gardner, Walter Little Gilmour (in the armchair), Lyne Stephens, the club servant, Sir Frederick Johnstone (at breakfast), Lord Rokeby (reading a newspaper), Lord Forester (by the fireplace), Lord Kinnaird (writing), Rowland Errington, for whom the painting was commissioned in 1839. Above the fireplace is depicted a painting by John Ferneley. It is presumed this is a record of a breakfast at The New Club opposite The George on High Street prior to a day's hunting with the Quorn.

The Prince of Wales at Sysonby in 1925. The sporting prince, who became Edward VIII in 1936, made Melton Mowbray one of his retreats from his official round of royal duties.

Sysonby Lodge in 1911. In the early nineteenth century this was the home of Frederick Ponsonby, 3rd Earl of Bessborough, Baron Ponsonby of Sysonby, whose daughter, Lady Caroline Lamb, was passionately infatuated with Lord Byron. On seeing his cortege being transported along Nottingham Road, Melton Mowbray to Hucknall Torkard, she collapsed and her mind became unbalanced. She never completely recovered.

Thorpe Arnold toll-gate. In 1856 William Brown, alias Peppermint Billy, murdered the gatekeeper, Edward Woodcock, aged 70 and his 10-year-old grandson, James. For this crime Brown was hanged in front of Welford Road prison, the last public hanging in Leicester.

The base of the medieval market cross near the church of St Mary, Thorpe Arnold.

Two

The Wreake Valley and Settlements to the North

Kirby Gate.

A meet of the Quorn Hunt in 1906 at Kirby Gate, Kirby Bellars, when Mrs Rippen was in residence. .

The Cottage, 1925, home of John Brodie Esq. in Kirby Bellars.

Kirby Lodge, 1920. The Woodward family with their turkeys at Kirby Bellars.

Kirby Lodge, 1921. Walter Woodward and Zillah Woodward with their children Laura, Bertha and Walter at Kirby Bellars.

The Flying Childers public house at Kirby Bellars in 1904, when John Walker was the licensee. The cottages shown are now a private house. The Childers is now a purpose-built public house further along the road. It was named after a racehorse owned by the 2nd Duke of Devonshire which, in 1719, was considered to be the finest racehorse in the world. A life-size portrait of the famous horse hangs in Chatsworth House, Derbyshire.

Main Street, Kirby Bellars, leading to the main Leicester road in 1916. To the right of the photograph stands the village post office. Miss Sarah Ann Randle was sub-postmistress.

A pleasant view of the church of St Mary, Ashby Folville in 1905. The vicar and rural dean was Revd John Godson MA of St Catherine's College, Cambridge. He was also rural dean for the Goscate Division.

The Carington Arms public house at Ashby Folville in 1916, when John Alfred Walker was the publican.

Ashby Folville windmill in 1939. It was built between 1815 and 1826 and Hercules Brown was miller in 1891.

Left: The remains of the tower at Ashby Folville in 1970, now used as an agricultural store.

Opposite above: Barsby post office in 1916. Albert Boden Platt, sub-postmaster and grocer, is standing in his shop doorway with family and friends. The building is now the Three Bows, a private house.

Opposite below: Bagrave End, Barsby, leading to Church Lane in 1906. Six Cottage Row is on the right of the photograph.

Barsby windmill in 1900, the remains of the post mill that ceased working in the late 1880s. Mr A. Greaves was miller in 1855.

Main Street, Gaddesby in 1916 with the Hermitage on the right.

Looking down Main Street, Gaddesby, toward the junction with Cross Street from outside of Hill Side in 1916.

The church of St Luke at Gaddesby in 1910, when the vicar was the Revd Richard Quarry MA of Trinity College, Dublin.

Re-thatching what is now No. 17 Main Street, Gaddesby in 1913. Opposite is the village blacksmith's forge.

The corner of Mill Lane and Great Lane, Frisby-on-the-Wreake in 1900. The thatched cottage to the right is now called Sunnyside Cottage.

A view of Main Street, Frisby-on-the-Wreake in 1900. The Black Horse public house is on the left. The landlord at that time was Austin Rodwell.

The market cross on Main Street, Frisby-on-the-Wreake in 1916. This view can be compared with the one below taken sixteen years earlier.

The market cross in Frisby-on-the-Wreake, 1900. To the left of the photograph is the workshop of Anthony and William Whitaker, saddlers.

The thatched cottage on Rotherby Lane, Frisby-on-the-Wreake in 1906. The cottage still stands showing very little alteration and is now called Zion House.

Main Street, Frisby-on-the-Wreake in 1904. A wheelbarrow stands outside the wheelwrights shop owned by Charles Edward Frisby. The sign for the Bell public house (licensee Robert Weston) is just visible in the centre background. On the right is the bakehouse run by Samuel Arthur Marriott.

Asfordby church and rectory in 1906. The vicar was the Revd John Charles Wellesley Burnaby MA of Trinity Hall, Cambridge.

Asfordby post office in 1936 when Thomas Charles Garland was postmaster. The adjacent tailors shop was run by Reginald Arthur Shilham.

The Primitive Methodist chapel, Asfordby in 1904. Built in 1840 and enlarged in 1884, it is now a butchers shop.

Asfordby Hall in 1928, the residence of Lady Theresa and Mr John Cross. In the 1960s the hall was converted to auction rooms and used by Mr Eric Startin. By 1970 the building had been demolished.

Main Street, Asfordby, April 1940, flooded by the waters of the Wreake.

Asfordby water-mill in 1932 just before it was demolished and the wheel sold for scrap. Tom Hives was the miller who ground corn in this water-mill in 1900.Asfordby water-mill in 1932 just before it was demolished and the wheel sold for scrap. Tom Hives was the miller who ground corn in this water-mill in 1900.

Asfordby water-mill in 1904 when George Adkins was the miller. The mill house to the right of the photograph was the home of the Charles family in the 1930s.

A huntsman in full pursuit, riding across the fields near Holwell Ironworks in 1926. A detail from a painting by Charles Simpson RI.

Holwell Ironworks, Melton Mowbray.

Holwell Ironworks, c. 1920. The foundations for the first blast furnace were laid down in 1878. This came about as a result of the discovery in 1874 of large quantities of iron-stone in the neighbouring villages of Holwell and Ab Kettleby by Mr Richard Dalgliesh. He formed the Holwell Iron Company in that year, naming it after the village of Holwell.

A dramatic photograph of Holwell works taken in the 1950s. The first furnace was blown in 1881. Eventually ironstone was mined in the villages of Buckminster, South Witham, Sewstern and Market Overton to name but a few.

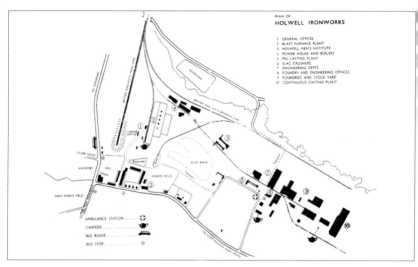

A plan of Holwell Ironworks.

Holwell Ironworks, 1950.

Shunting wagons at Holwell works containing scrap iron, prior to it being processed into pipes or metal inspection covers in 1969.

A view from the top of one of the furnaces at Holwell works in 1956 showing slag wagons in the background. A by-product of furnace production was crushed slag, graded and coated with tar, used as a road-surfacing aggregate. In 1950 3,000 tons per week were produced.

Holwell Works football team, 1951. Back row, left to right: Bert Perry, Walter Gunby, Jock Kerr, Dave Thomas, Derek Hack, Geoff Spiby. Front row: Raynor Garner, Vic Wright, Jimmy Learmonth, Bill Caithness, Norman Baxter.

Three Scotsmen playing for Holwell Works FC in the early 1950s. Left to right: Jimmy Learmonth, John Jardine, Bill Caithness.

The Army Dog Training Scheme kennels where the Royal Army Veterinary Corps dog training establishment was based at Welby.

'The Remount' at Welby, the army training camp for dogs and horses.

High Street, Ab Kettleby in 1910, looking towards the main Nottingham road.

Church Lane in 1904 at Ab Kettleby with the spire of the church of St James just showing above the trees. The living was then held by the Revd Thomas Caleb Hughes of St Aidan's.

Above: The elementary school, Ab Kettleby in 1910. Headmaster John Needham is standing to the right of a group of his pupils.

Right: The headmaster of Ab Kettleby school, Mr John Needham, with his family in 1905.

The seven-arched pack-horse bridge at Rearsby in 1906, showing the ford in the foreground.

Old Hall at Rearsby in 1900, the seat of Henry Valentine Story Esq.

Station Lane in 1916. In the centre background stands Rearsby station with the signal box that controlled the level crossing just visible through the trees. Herbert J. Roberts was the station master.

Church Lane in 1916 at Rearsby, leading to the church of St Michael. The vicar was the Revd Thomas Lionel George Hassall MA of Jesus College, Cambridge, and the sexton was Gordon Woodward.

Mill Road, Rearsby c. 1925. The thatched cottage with a horse and cart standing in front of it is now No. 31.

Church Leys in 1916 at Rearsby, the seat of Sir Hugo Meynell FitzHerbert Bt.

An Auster Aircraft Mk III manufactured by British Taylorcraft of Rearsby in 1943. This particular aircraft was on active duty with the British Eighth Army in Italy for artillery observation and liaison up to 19 July 1945.

Administrative buildings off Gaddesby Road, Rearsby, as used by Taylorcraft.

A meet of the Quorn hounds on the front lawn of Brooksby Hall in 1906. The hall was the home of Captain Gordon Chesney Wilson and Lady Sarah Spencer.

The head gardener's cottage at Brooksby Hall in 1906, the year the estate passed from the Wilson family to the Beattys, when it was purchased by Mrs Ethel Tree who married David Beatty.

Admiral of the Fleet Sir David Beatty in 1920 at the age of 49. He was the British Commander at the Battle of Jutland when the German fleet was routed on the 31 May 1916.

Brooksby Hall in 1910, the residence of Rear Admiral Sir David Beatty CB, MVO, DSO.

The Hall gardens in 1910 with the church of St Michael in the background. Sir David Beatty on his retirement from the navy was created an earl and chose the title Baron Beatty of the North Sea and Brooksby.

The church of All Saints, Rotherby in 1904. The vicar was the Revd Edward Aden Beresford BA, LLM of King's College, Cambridge who resided at Hoby. Lady Sarah Wilson lived in the rectory next to the church.

Main Street, Rotherby c. 1920. The gentleman holding the bicycle is standing in front of what is now No. 22.

The Hall at Rotherby in 1904, the home of Mrs Bell.

Rotherby Hall in 1925, now the home of John Cross Esq.

Hoby water-mill in 1874; a detail from a coloured print by John Sturgess. Lord Grey de Wilton, Mr G. Moore and the Revd Weller attempted to cross the plank bridge to the disused water-mill and splashed down into the River Wreake, so interrupting the hunt with the Quorn hounds being led by Tom Firr on Monday 16 February.

A general view of the village of Hoby from the Brooksby Road in 1904. In the centre background is the church of All Saints, where the vicar was the Revd Edward Aden Beresford MA, and the sexton John Mathers.

Cottages in front of the church of All Saints at Hoby, 1900. The ivy-clad cottage in the centre of the picture is now No. 26, Sunny Bank, and the thatched cottage to the right is Lovat Cottage, No. 16.

The elementary school at Hoby, 1916 when Charles Wheatley was headmaster. The school was built in 1871.

Shoby Priory, farmed by Thomas Hallam in the 1940s.

Shoby House, farmed by George Hobill in the 1940s.

The Stocks, Grimston in 1910.

The elementary school at Grimston, in 1916. Mrs Annie Johnson was headmistress.

The church of St John, Grimston, with the Bishop and Sharpe tombstones positioned in one line.

The Black Horse public house and the post office, Grimston in 1916. Arthur Wardle was the publican and William Botterill sub-postmaster.

The Park at Saxelby, 1904, the imposing residence of Charles William Wright Esq. JP.

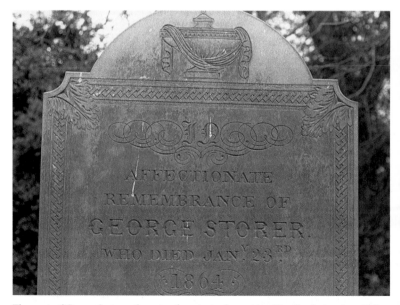

The grave of George Storer, a farmer and grazier in the parish of Saxelby during the middle of the nineteenth century, who died on 23 January 1864 aged 48 years.

The church of St Michael at Wartnaby, annexed to Ab Kettleby, viewed through the branches of an ancient fallen walnut tree. The vicar in the 1940s was the Revd John Clulow Thompson.

The dovecot near the church at Wartnaby.

Ragdale Hall, 1900, the home of the Hon. Alan Joseph Pennington and formerly the seat of the Earls Ferrers.

A general view of the village of Ragdale in 1904. The elementary school was maintained at the sole expense of Duke Storza-Cesarini. Miss Mary Skinner was headmistress and George Hamson was parish clerk.

School Lane, now Main Road, Old Dalby in 1916. The elementary school (now the village hall) is on the right. Thomas M. Hingley was headmaster. The cottage on the left is now called April Cottage.

Horses grazing on the village green at Old Dalby in 1904, seven years after the sapling standing in front of the ivy-clad cottage (background, right) was planted to commemorate the Diamond Jubilee of Queen Victoria. This tree, a Spanish oak, has flourished and now has a trunk 4 ft across and dominates this area of the village.

Church Lane, Old Dalby in 1916, with the church of St Martin in the middle distance. The sexton was Robert Peel.

St Martin's church in 1925, when the living was held by the Revd Reginald Sydney Carruthers Hawthorn Wood MA of St John's College, Cambridge. To the left of the photograph is the private entrance to Old Dalby Hall which, in 1925, was the seat of Charles James Phillips Esq. DL, JP. He was a principal shareholder in Watneys Brewery and was regularly conveyed through these gates in a 'coach and four'.

Chapel Lane, Nether Broughton in 1900, named after the Wesleyan chapel built in 1839.

Nether Broughton post office in 1904, looking from King Street. Charles George Milnes was sub-postmaster. This thatched post office has long since been demolished but the present post office is situated next door in the row of terraced houses.

The church of St Mary at Nether Broughton with the memorial to the village lads who gave their lives in the First World War.

The Anchor Inn on the main Nottingham road, Nether Broughton in 1936, when Tom Crook was the licensee.

Three

The Burrough Escarpment
and Settlements to the South

The Green, Top End, Great Dalby in 1910, with the church of St Swithin in the background. The Revd Robert Carthew Dashwood MA was vicar, the sexton was Joel Sharpe.

Above left and right: Coats of arms high up on the south side of St Swithin's, Great Dalby. On the left, quartered three lions of England, passant and the fleur-de-lis of France, ancient and modern. Right, Thomas de Brotherton, Earl of Norfolk.

Eye Kettleby water-mill, c. 1850. The mill ceased operating during the First World War and was purchased and demolished by the district council in the 1920s so that they could control the water rights.

A detail from a painting by Rigby Graham, 1969, of the remains of the bomb aiming tower which was part of the training area on Great Dalby Aerodrome.

Left: LAC Jack Williamson, stationed at Dalby Aerodrome. In 1944 he was awarded a life-saving certificate for assisting in the rescue of the crew of a plane which crashed off Saxby Road, Melton Mowbray at Copley's South, now an industrial estate.

Below: A view of the control tower at Dalby Aerodrome in 1967. This tower, built as an experimental unit, was unique in the whole of Britain. It should never have been demolished in the 1970s.

Opposite above: The successful RAF football team that represented Melton Mowbray (Dalby Aerodrome) in the 1943/4 season. Back row, left to right: MacDonald, Casson, Reg David, -?-, -?-, Fred Butcher. Front row: Bill Gould, Jimmy Learmonth, Bert Broadhurst, Fred Moon, Jack Smith.

Opposite below: Three RAF personnel in 1944 near the hanger that stood adjacent to Great Dalby village. Left to right: Jimmy Learmonth, Ian Hunter and their friend Alan.

The grandstand for the 1900 Burton races. As is apparent from the photograph, this was a highly fashionable venue, nobility patronizing the event.

The ring at Burton races in 1912. Lord Glentanor resided at the manor house nearby.

Thorpe Satchville Hall in 1905, owned by John Otho Paget and occupied by Henry Harrison Parry and F.H.K. Durlacher.

The Pinfold, Thorpe Satchville.

The Pinfold, Thorpe Satchville in 1905, owned by Frederick Kneeling Durlacher.

Little Dalby Hall, 1904, the residence of Mrs Burns-Hartopp, lady of the manor, and her husband Capt. James Burns-Hartopp JP, MFH.

Little Dalby Hall, 1903. This hall, built in the Elizabethan period, was extensively restored in 1838 and 1851. This photograph was used as a postcard, and on the reverse is the comment that the sender is about to commence making the Stilton cheese for Christmas.

White House Farm on the junction of Loseby Lane and Burrough Road, Twyford, 1905.

Main Road, Twyford in 1910, with Brook House on the left and the cheese dairy in the middle distance, which was demolished during the Second World War by a runaway army lorry.

Town Bridge on Main Road, Twyford c. 1905.

Main Street, Twyford in 1910 with the Odd Fellows Hall, built in 1908, on the right. It is now the village hall.

The edge of the escarpment of Burrough Hill, 690 ft above sea level. The hill is the site of an Iron Age encampment.

Main Street, Burrough on the Hill, leading to Somerby, in 1910.

The church of St Mary at Burrough on the Hill with the rectory in the foreground, 1916. The rector was the Revd John M. Gedan MA.

The junction with Main Street and Newbold gated road, Burrough on the Hill in 1910. The entrance to Burrough House is in the background, to the left.

Ashleigh House on Main Street, Somerby in 1905.

Somerby House.

Somerby House in 1905, occupied by Charles Edward Hay Esq.

The Grove, Somerby in 1905, when it was occupied by Major Augustus Candy.

High Street, Somerby c. 1950. A girl on a pony is standing outside the village school with the local garage in the centre background.

Stooks of corn standing in 'Red-earth' Pickwell in the 1920s.

Pickwell war memorial, c. 1950.

All Saints' church, Pickwell, viewed from the rectory garden in 1910.

The rectory at Pickwell in 1908. The Revd Charles James Petne Blundell MA was the incumbent.

The north side of Leesthorpe Hall in 1908, the seat of Francis Sloane Stanley Esq. DL, JP.

Cottesmore hounds at a meet in the park on the south side of Leesthorpe Hall in 1928. The Hall was then the seat of John W. Burns Esq. JP. The Master of Fox Hounds was James Baird Esq.

The junction to Knossington and Somerby, Cold Overton in 1905.

Cold Overton Hall in 1916, the seat of James F. Montagu Esq.

Frederick Holmes' farm cart standing on the Somerby Road, Cold Overton in 1925.

The gated road to Whissendine, Cold Overton in 1905.

The Greyhound public house, Knossington in 1906. Mrs Martha Weatherstone was the licensee.

The elementary school, Knossington in 1906, erected in 1899 by A.L. Duncan Esq. for £1,500.
In 1906 Archie Looker was headmaster, and Miss Susan Weatherstone the infants mistress.

'Whalebones' on Main Street, Knossington in 1916.

The entrance to 'Whalebones' opposite the Braunston Road on Main Street, Knossington in 1905. On the left is the home of farmer and grazier Evan Louis Evans Esq.

Knossington Mill in 1895 when William Gale was the miller. This tower mill was erected in 1849 by Mr E. Clarke.

The remains of Knossington Mill in 1970 when the base was being used as a farm store. No trace of this mill now exists.

Four

Along the River Eye

Left: The headstone over the grave of Robert Thorpe Chamberlain in the graveyard of St Mary the Virgin at Wyfordby. He was parish clerk for thirty-three years and sub-postmaster up until his death in 1893 aged 80.

Below: Gangers' 'bothy' at Brentingby in the spring of 1965.

Above: Greengate ford bridge over the River Eye at Brentingby, 1966. This was constructed by the Oakham Canal Company in the 1790s to carry horse-drawn vehicles over the river to the adjacent bridge that spanned the Melton to Oakham canal. For very many years it was maintained by the Midland Railway Company.

Right: Brentingby crossing gatehouse on the edge of the Peterborough to Nottingham railway in 1933. The crossing keeper was responsible for opening the crossing gates on the field road leading to Greengate ford bridge and the polo ground beyond. In the 1920s and '30s this was a 'mecca' for the royalty and nobility who spent the season in the Melton Mowbray district supporting the three local hunts.

Left: The church of St Mary in the winter of 1947. Freeby village was cut off from the outside world for nearly six weeks because of drifting snow.

Below: Graham and Pamela Mason sitting on a farm dray at the boundary fence to 'Beckam's' at Freeby in the autumn of 1947.

Above: An aerial view of farm buildings and Brook Cottages at the east end of Freeby village in the late 1960s.

Right: Pamela Mason with her 'cade' lamb, a familiar sight on Freeby main street during the summer of 1949.

The thatched cottage on the Garthorpe road, Saxby in the 1920s. Charlie Skerritt is on the right and his daughter Fanny is on the far left of the group. This picturesque building was demolished by Buckminster Estates many years ago.

His Majesty King Edward VII standing on Saxby station on the Nottingham– Peterborough line, in 1907, waiting for his Sandringham connection.

Right: Alice Smith of Saxby in 1927. Note the necklace of hand-marbled wooden beads.

Below: Abram Smith servicing his steam traction engine at Saxby in 1925.

Left: Mile post on the towpath of the Melton to Oakham canal near Saxby in 1965. This canal was opened in 1803 and closed in 1847 when it was purchased by the Midland Railway Company.

Below: Alice Smith and Bill Mason haymaking in the summer of 1926 at Saxby.

Roasting an ox at Garthorpe in the paddock at the junction of the Coston to Saxby road in 1897 to celebrate the Diamond Jubilee of Queen Victoria.

Castle mound and ditch on the edge of the River Eye at Garthorpe in 1969. These defensive earthworks, with water-filled ditch and palisade of sharpened stakes, were 'thrown up' throughout the country as a matter of expedience during the anarchic reign of Stephen (1135–54) and relied chiefly on their height and the strength of the earthern ramparts.

Coston water-mill in the 1890s. Remains of this mill can still be seen next to the ford on the Sproxton road.

The blue brick bridge over the River Eye at Coston. The brick cottage in the background was built by the Earl of Dysart in 1884.

Main Street, Buckminster, 1904. Thompson Skins stands outside his blacksmiths shop with his assistant and several onlookers. In the background on the left stands the Dysart Arms Hotel. Arthur Wells was the proprietor.

William (Trump) Farley at the controls of his locomotive pulling loaded wagons off the edge of the opencast ironstone working near Buckminster cricket ground in the 1950s.

Buckminster Hall in 1916, erected in 1798 and the seat of the Earl of Dysart. It was demolished in the 1950s and a new hall has been built on the site.

The entrance to the stables at Buckminster Hall in 1904, part of the estate owned by the Earl of Dysart. William Weston was harness maker to the earl.

Loading ironstone with a drag line into wagons near the Colsterworth road, Buckminster in 1956.

Sharon Hickman of Wymondham on George Slack's pony at Buckminster Gymkhana in 1964.

The Bede Houses near the River Eye at Stapleford in 1939. The buildings were extensively restored in 1992.

Jack Pickaver, blacksmith, repairing a pump in the forge at Stapleford in 1965. Harry Oliver is on the bellows, keeping up the heat so necessary for good ironwork production.

The two principal actors from The Avengers of ABC Television making a film in Stapleford Park in 1965. The Hall is in the background, the lake is on the left, and John Steed (Patrick MacNee) is untying Emma Peel (Diana Rigg) in the nick of time to save her from a gruesome death at the hands of villains of the foulest kind.

A working model of the SS *Northern Star* cruising on the lake in Stapleford Park in the summer of 1963.

The main entrance to Stapleford Hall in 1925, the seat of Lieut.-Col. John Gretton CBE, VD, MP, JP, lord of the manor.

Peter Pepper with his Priestman Dragline excavator, prior to his partially cleaning out the lake in 1958 using an 8 cu. ft bucket in Stapleford Park.

The Three Horse Shoes public house on the main street, Wymondham in 1904, when the publican was Daniel Burton.

The Rookery at Wymondham in 1916, the residence of John P. Grenfell Esq.

Edmondthorpe and Wymondham railway station in 1904 when John Cook was the station master. The spire of the church of St Peter can be seen in the background. The vicar at the time was the Revd William Hill Lee MA of Christ's College, Cambridge.

A Midland and Great Northern Johnson 4-4-0 in Wymondham railway station in 1937 waiting for passengers to board.

WYMONDHAM MILL

W.Till. Photo.

Above: Wymondham windmill in 1904.
Thomas Oldham was the miller.

Right: The millstone floor in Wymondham
Windmill in 1970, seen during the extensive
restoration programme.

Sycamore House at Wymondham in 1904, then the residence of Richard Louis Fenwick who was married to the actress Sylvia Gray. Just visible to the left is the oak tree planted in 1887 to commemorate Queen Victoria's Golden Jubilee.

Wymondham Odd Fellows Club parade outside the Hunters Arms in 1900. Mr George Duffin is standing at the horse's head. The passengers on the Ellis and Everard's delivery dray are, left to right: Mrs Curtis (when a child), Mrs Townsend, Esther Naylor, Lucy Bellamy, S. Saunders, -?-, Marjorie Ward, E. Pickaver. The publican of the Hunters Arms was Edward Charles Saunders.

Above: Wymondham Dairy, 1910, manufacturers of fine Stilton cheese. Left to right: Mrs Bratby, Miss Briggs, Mrs W. Harris, Miss S. Chafer (manageress).

Right: The headstone of Samuel Pears in Wymondham churchyard, positioned a few yards west of the church tower. Known as 'the Rag Man's Grave', this headstone was erected at the expense of Revd Richard Cragg who also wrote the poem engraved upon the stone. Samuel Pears was married four times and was a legend in his own lifetime.

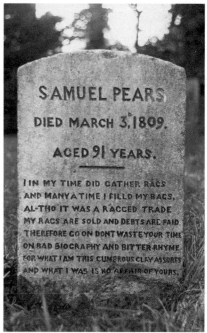

SAMUEL PEARS

DIED MARCH 3, 1809.

AGED 91 YEARS.

I IN MY TIME DID GATHER RAGS
AND MANY A TIME I FILLD MY BAGS,
AL-THO IT WAS A RAGGED TRADE
MY RAGS ARE SOLD AND DEBTS ARE PAID.
THEREFORE GO ON DONT WASTE YOUR TIME
ON BAD BIOGRAPHY AND BITTER RHYME.
FOR WHAT I AM THIS CUMBROUS CLAY ASSURES
AND WHAT I WAS IS NO AFFAIR OF YOURS.

Inside the control gondola of the Schütte-Lanz airship of the German Imperial Army that bombed Paines railway sidings, in the parish of Wymondham, on 3 September 1916.

The goods yard at Wymondham railway station in 1918. The people at the depot of Herbert Whait, coal merchant of Melton Mowbray are, left to right: Robert Barfoot (Whait's agent in Wymondham), Henry Naylor (horseman, sitting), Tom Fisher (horseman, standing).

The Blue Dog public house on the main street, Sewstern in 1916. The publican was Thomas Arthur Wilson.

School Lane at Sewstern in 1916. On the left of the photograph stands Brook Cottages, built in 1913, and behind this building stands Grange House, built in 1893. The row of cottages on the right has been demolished.

The Wesleyan chapel at Sewstern in 1916. The chapel was built in 1904 at a cost of £600.v

'Jason' in the loco sheds situated off Gunby Road at Sewstern in 1966.

The hollow elm tree standing in front of Edmondthorpe post office in 1904 when Miss Emma Worsdale was sub-postmistress. In the background on the right stands the elementary school erected in 1838 and extensively rebuilt at the expense of William Ann Pochin Esq. in 1863. The headmistress was Miss Edith Ellen Booth.

The only surviving bridge on the Melton to Oakham canal, 1965. This bridge originally carried vehicles on the road from Teigh to Edmondthorpe; now it is just an access point to two fields.

Above: School House at Edmondthorpe in 1907, then the home of Miss Edith Ellen Booth, headmistress of the elementary school.

Left: The gardens of School House at Edmondthorpe in 1907. Miss Edith Ellen Booth sits in the front of the group and her brother, Syd Booth, stands at the back.

Above: Clearing snow on the Wymondham to Edmondthorpe road in 1947. From left to right: Mr Jack Welbourn, Mr E. Veasey, Mr Gerry Potter, Mr A. Pepper. The roads in this parish were completely blocked by drifting snow for seven weeks.

Right: The decorated font in the church of St Michael and All Angels at Edmondthorpe in 1965. The vicar was the Revd John Lawrence Vincent Houghton.

The Smith monument in Edmondthorpe church. The lower alabaster figure is Lady Ann Smith; the effigy has a red stain on the left wrist and under certain circumstances is said to 'bleed'. She was considered to be a witch and capable of turning herself into a white cat. The white cat was caught thieving in the kitchen by the cook and its left paw was slashed with a cleaver. From that day onwards the lady of the house carried a red scar on her left wrist.

Edmondthorpe Hall in 1791, the seat of William Pochin Esq., from an engraving by John Throsby.

Edmondthorpe Hall in 1904, the residence of Victoria Alexandrina, Dowager Countess of Yarborough and John Maunsell-Richardson Esq.

The remains of Edmondthorpe Hall in 1965. The magnificent Hall was burnt down in 1943 while occupied by German prisoners of war; the result of an incident in the kitchen with the army cook, a white cat, a candle and a pan of fat!

Whissendine station, Edmondthorpe. A photograph of a colour print by John Sturgess involving the Cottesmore Hunt on 20 March 1879. Ignoring the pleas of the crossing keeper, Captain Stirling, Mr George Finch and others decided to take a short cut to Wymondham Roughs along the railway, with disastrous results.

Whissendine station on the Peterborough to Nottingham railway line near Edmonsthorpe in 1965. The half-timbered ticket office has now been demolished.

Five

Towards the Vale of Belvoir and High Leicestershire

The junction of Hose Lane with Waltham Lane, Long Clawson in 1904. Elms Farm lies directly behind the signpost, with Sunnycroft to the right of the photograph.

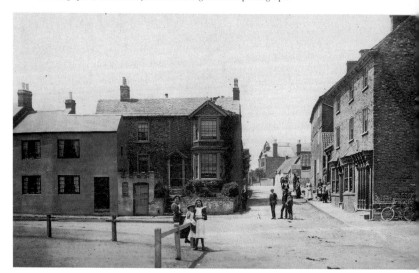

The centre of the east end of the village of Long Clawson in 1904. The Sands is to the right of the photograph. Pack House on the left had only just been built. The house in the centre is Lynwood and the shop across the road on the right is now Lumb and Co., Butchers.

Long Clawson windmill in 1935, a six-storeyed brick tower mill built in the early 1800s on the site of an earlier mill. John Henry Shilcock was the miller in 1916. It ceased working as a windmill during the First World War.

A parking area off The Sands, Long Clawson c. 1902. The house on the left has now been demolished and the village surgery is built on the site. The post office, which was run by John Bissell Millar, can be seen behind the parish notice-board. Mr Millar also ran the bakery next door.

The Crown and Plough at Long Clawson in 1904, when Albine Knapp was the publican. He was also the carrier to Nottingham on Saturday and Melton Mowbray on Tuesday. The cottage on the right has been demolished and the village hall now stands on the site.

Long Clawson Dairy Ltd in 1932. The dairy, managed by William McNair, manufactured prime Stilton cheese.

The Wesleyan chapel at Long Clawson in 1932. The chapel was built in 1840 and stands next door to the manse, where the Wesleyan vicar, the Revd John Wesley Thornley lived.

The church of St Remigius, Long Clawson in 1932. The vicar was the Revd George Douglas Jordan BA of Leeds University. This photograph also shows the Primitive Methodist chapel built in 1868.

West End Stores, Long Clawson in 1932.

The church of St Michael, Hose in 1904, when the Revd John Williams of St Bees was the vicar. In the centre of the photograph stands the elementary school built in 1845. Henry Martin was headmaster.

The Baptist chapel, Long Clawson in 1928. It was built in 1818 and was licensed for marriages.

The church of St Michael viewed from the village green in Hose in 1936. The living was held by the Revd Frederick Appleton of University College, Durham.

The bridge over the Grantham Canal at Hose in 1928. William Jessop presented a bill to Parliament in 1792 to construct a canal from Nottingham to Grantham. After many difficulties had been overcome, the whole length of the canal was opened for navigation in 1797.

The Methodist chapel, Harby in 1904, built in 1847.

The elementary school at Hose was erected in 1860 and could accommodate 120 boys and girls. It is pictured here in 1904 when Alfred Warman Edwards was headmaster.

Harby village, c. 1938, with the war memorial to the lads of the village who gave their lives in the First World War and the village school built in 1860.

Dickman's Lane, Harby in the 1960s. The converted cottages on this lane are now named Trevelyans Cottage.

Right: Harby windmill in 1900. Messrs Lamin and Shipman were the millers, grinding corn and manufacturing cattle-cake for local use.

Below: An interior view of the stone floor inside Harby mill in 1939 showing a pair of stones. In 1937 the mill was purchased by Dickman and Wolley who ground pig and cattle feed for their own use and for sale to local farmers. In 1938 the mill was 'tail-winded'; it was not repaired and the owners sold the machinery for scrap. When Langer Aerodrome was built the mill was in the direct flight path and the top two floors were therefore removed.

The Red Lion on Red Lion Street, Stathern, viewed from the Toft in 1904. Thomas Hart was the publican.

Thatched cottages off The Green, Stathern in 1904. All these buildings have now been demolished except for Peck's Homestead, the last cottage in the row on the left.

A signal box on the railway sidings at Stathern serving the local opencast mines in 1966.

Looking towards Bottesford from Stathern ironstone railway sidings in 1966.

The church of St Guthlac, Stathern in 1904, when the vicar was the Revd John William Taylor MA, JP of St Peter's College, Cambridge. Laburnam House is the white house in the centre, with Mill House to the left.

The remains of the base of Stathern post mill in 1955. The wooden body of the mill had been removed before 1900, and the roundhouse has now been completely demolished. The last recorded millers were William Rowten and Robert Starbuck in 1892.

The entrance to the ironstone mine at Holwell in 1885.

The ancient chapelry at Holwell with one bell. The vicar of Ab Kettleby would officiate at services here.

A general view of Scalford in 1900. The church of St Egelwin the Martyr is in the centre background. The vicar was the Revd Henry Twells Mogridge MA of St Peter's College, Cambridge, and the sexton was Benjamin Pearson. William Wilford Whittle was clerk to the parish council. Scalford Dairy, producer of fine Stilton cheese, is in the foreground.

The Primitive Methodist chapel built in 1870 and viewed from King Street, Scalford in 1904. Further down the street is the Kings Arms, where James Watchorn was the publican and, in the middle distance, The Plough, where the publican was Richard Graves Pollard.

The headstone of John Morris's grave in Scalford churchyard. He lived at the Manor House, Wymondham, and was buried in the family plot at Scalford. The Morris family were farmers and cheese manufacturers, John's nephew successfully running the Wymondham Dairy, producer of fine Stilton cheese.

Scalford station in the 1930s, a class J39 train passing through on the way to Leicester. Stilton cheese was conveyed direct to the House of Commons in London via this station prior to the Second World War.

Church Street, Scalford in 1900. The imposing building to the left of centre is the post office, William Wright the sub-postmaster.

The Wesleyan chapel, Scalford in 1904. This large chapel was built in 1844.

The undenominational mission room erected in 1896 at Wycomb.

The chapel of St Mary, Wycomb, built before 1300 in the Norman style in the fields at Chadwell.

Goadby Hall in 1900, the seat of Lady Henrietta Turner and Algernon Turner Esq. CB, JP at Goadby Marwood. Their farm bailiff was William Moseley.

The school at Goadby Marwood, erected in 1861 at a cost of £350, was paid for by a former rector of the church of St Denys.

The approach to Eastwell village in the 1950s.

A sign indicating Eastwell Quarries in 1966.

The engine sheds at Eastwell Quarries on top of Harby Hill in 1966. The rails ran down to Stathern ironstone railway sidings.

A cable-operated incline at Eastwell in 1959 conveying iron ore from the quarries to the British Rail main railhead and sidings.

A general view of Eaton in 1916, with the embattled Norman tower of St Denis sitting high on the skyline. The vicar was the Revd James Henry Moore MA of Durham University, and the parish clerk was Thomas Pearson.

Eaton Grange in 1916, the seat of Major George C.B. Paynter DSO.

'Rutland' standing in the mineral railway sidings at Eaton before the First World War.

A British Rail branch line, showing the timber viaduct near Eaton in 1955.

'Nantes' in full steam near Eaton in 1955. Built in France, this engine came to the Waltham Quarries in 1934.

Two locals standing outside The Wheel Inn, Branston in 1904 when Miss Ann Hand was the publican. In the centre background two people can just be discerned. They are Harry Clifford and Mrs George.

Branston church in 1928. The living from the church of St Guthlac is annexed to Croxton Kerrial whose vicar was the Revd John Henry Evans BA of St David's College, Lampeter. Stephen Malcolm Pilkington was living in the rectory, which is now covered in ivy and looks very different from the photograph on the next page. An alcove in the church wall holds the recently installed war memorial.

The elementary school at Branston, erected in 1843. Miss Orpah Murrell was headmistress when this photograph was taken in 1916.

Branston Rectory in 1906. The vicar for the parish was the Revd David Vilkie Peregrine BA, LTh of University College, Durham, appointed in 1905. He was also rural dean for the Framland division.

The crossroads in the centre of Waltham-on-the-Wolds in 1904. The Royal Horse Shoes public house, whose licensee was William Edwin Rose, is on the right.

Melton Road, Waltham-on-the-Wolds in 1916. The spire of the church of St Mary Magdalene is just visible above the trees. The vicar was the Revd Bertell Hubert Smith MA of Durham University, and the parish clerk and sexton was William Clark. On the left are the stone pillars indicating the entrance to the elementary school, erected in 1844; George Higgens was headmaster at the time of the photograph.

The windmill at Waltham-on-the-Wolds in 1925, when the miller was Edward Robinson. This mill was built on the site of a post mill in 1868. The Robinson family had been millers and ground corn in mills on this site continuously for over 100 years. It was sold to Richard and Walter Owen in the 1920s.

Above left: The spur wheel driving the stone-nut, 1938.

Above right: The feed leading to the millstone, 1938.

High Street, Waltham-on-the-Wolds 1916. The house on the right is Stoneleigh and the sign of The Wheel public house is just visible at the end of the roadway. The licensee in 1916 was Mrs Sarah Ann Lock.

Waltham-on-the-Wolds signal box on the Great Northern branch line from Scalford in the 1940s. This was mainly a goods line, but when the Croxton Park racecourse was in full use a passenger service was introduced solely for the event.

An ancient drinking trough for cattle and horses at the entrance to Race Course Farm, Bescaby.

The gable end of a typical cottage built in the nineteenth century for farm workers and their families at Bescaby.

A general view of Croxton Kerrial in 1904, with the church of St John the Baptist in the middle distance. The vicar at the time was the Revd William Ernest Pelham Malden BA of Trinity College, Cambridge. The parish clerk was William Charity.

Main Street, Croxton Kerrial in 1916. Charles John Prowse was headmaster at the elementary school, built in 1844. Miss Laura Prowse and Miss Letitia Adams were assistants. The Peacock Inn stands at the end of the street. Robert Knott was the publican.

Croxton Kerrial smock mill in 1905. In the foreground is the last miller, Newman Shire, busy feeding his hens and turkeys.

Croxton Kerrial village in 1905, with the parish pump in the centre foreground. The smock mill in the background would appear to be unique as it was the only one built in this style in Leicestershire. It had a boat-shaped cap.

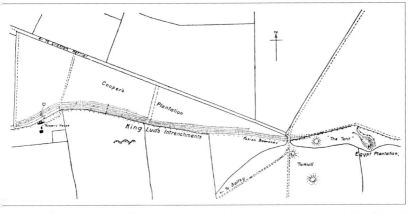

King Lud's entrenchments. This defence system stretches for about three-quarters of a mile along the parish boundary with Saltby. It is a ditch and rampart fortification to defend a kingdom against advancing armies. Legend ascribes it to the Bronze Age, some 3,000 years ago, when King Lud was involved in what can only be described as 'trench warfare'.

The centre of Stonesby in 1904. The church of St Peter stands high in the background. The vicar of Waltham-on-the-Wolds held the living, and the parish clerk was Thomas Bursnall. Henry Hickman ran the grocers and drapers shop near the church.

A typical red pantiled roof so common in this area of Leicestershire. The tower behind is that of St Peter's church, Stonesby.

The Nags Head public house standing at the crossroads in the centre of Saltby in 1904. Alfred Henry Skinner was the publican; he also ran the local shop.

High Street, Saltby in 1916. The Nags Head public house is on the right, where Townsend Pretty was the publican.

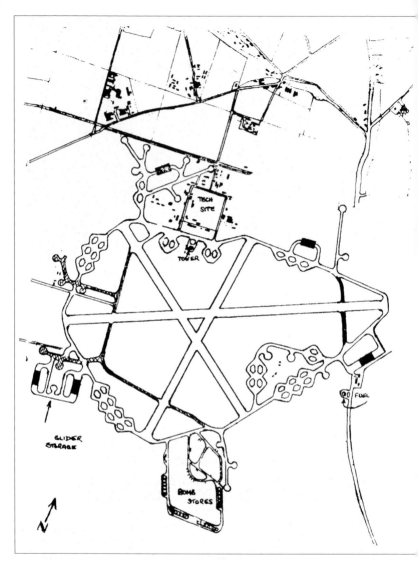

TECH SITE

TOWER

FUEL

GLIDER STORAGE

N

BOMB STORES

A plan of Saltby Aerodrome, a satellite of Cottesmore. Built in the early 1940s, it was a base for the American Air Force who flew Flying Fortresses out of it on many successful raids on occupied Europe. It was also one of the many aerodromes that were staging bases for the glider invasion of northern France in support of the D-Day landings.

A detail from a line and wash illustration by Rigby Graham, 1969, showing the remains of the bomb aiming tower which was part of the training area on Saltby aerodrome.

The main control tower on Saltby Aerodrome, 1969.

The squadron insignia made by American airmen in the 1940s on the approach road to Saltby Aerodrome in 1970. The roadside verge where it lay has since been altered.

Gliders on Saltby Aerodrome, now part of the aerial scene in this part of Leicestershire.

The elementary school, Sproxton in 1916, when the headmaster was Francis Joseph Warham. The school was built in 1871 for 100 children. It has since been converted into the village hall.

The post office, Sproxton in 1916 when Ernest Harry Trayford was sub-postmaster and grocer. The Crown public house is visible to the left of centre in the background. Henry Joel Tarratt was the publican.

British Rail line to Sproxton Quarries, looking down the line from Crabtree Lane bridge in 1966.

Carvings on the Saxon cross that stands in the graveyard at the church of St Bartholomew, Sproxton.

Sproxton post mill in the early 1920s.
J. Pridmore was the miller in 1916.
It stopped work in 1920 and was
demolished in 1949 to make way for the
Sproxton opencast iron ore workings.

The brake wheel, windshaft and stone-
nut inside Sproxton post mill in 1939.

Acknowledgements

To compile a book of this type would not be possible without the help of many kind and well disposed individuals. The basis of this collection of old photographs has been the author's own extensive collection, and it is presumed that all the photographs from this source are out of copyright. Should this not be the case, Trevor Hickman offers his sincere apologies for reproducing them without permission and will make an acknowledgement in future publications. Collections such as his are made over very many years and, first and foremost, the author thanks his wife Pamela for her continued patience for over thirty years spent with a passionate collector of local history ephemera and publications. Inspiration came from many sources and the author's good friend, the artist Rigby Graham, has provided considerable help over the years. He allowed the author to use photographs taken by him and to reproduce two photographs of his paintings, one of which is in the collection of Mike Goldmark. Nigel Moon, the enthusiastic miller, would have filled the book with photographs of mills, mill machinery and mineral railway lines with locomotives in full steam. Many of the photographs showing these subjects have been provided by Nigel. Photographs of Holwell Works and information are from the author's late father-in-law, Bill Mason, with whom he spent many enjoyable hours discussing local industry and farming in this area of Leicestershire. Thanks are due to Mr and Mrs A. Charles for their professional help over many years and also for allowing the author to reproduce photographs of Asfordby, Kirby Bellars and Melton Mowbray extracted from their private collection. David Burton of Stroud provided information on Melton families; unfortunately, due to lack of space, only one photograph has been reproduced. Chris Salter of Midland Counties Publications found the photograph of the Auster aircraft reproduced on p. 49. Lady Gretton has very kindly allowed the reproduction of photographs taken by her late husband, John, of interesting features associated with Stapleford Park. Jimmy Learmonth provided considerable information on Dalby Aerodrome and uncovered many photographs of football teams associated with this aerodrome and with Holwell Works. The Squire de Lisle found the photograph of the Prince of Wales, reproduced on p. 19, in his extensive collection. Thanks are also due to all those people in so many villages that the author visited in the spring of 1992 who willingly offered advice and help in identifying the sites depicted in many of the photographs. Finally, thanks to Jenny Weston, who converted the author's awful handwritten text into a neat typescript for the publisher.